Love and War

Contemporary
Kurdish Women Poets

Love and War
Contemporary
Kurdish Women Poets

edited by Maram al-Masri
translated by Alan Dent

smoke

**STACK
BOOKS**

Smokestack Books
School Farm
Nether Silton
Thirsk
North Yorkshire
YO7 2JZ

e-mail: info@smokestack-books.co.uk

www.smokestack-books.co.uk

first published as *La Poèsie des femmes kurdes*
(Le Merle Moqueur, Paris, 2023).
Poems copyright the authors, 2023.

English translations
copyright Alan Dent 2024.
All rights reserved.

ISBN 9781739473426

Smokestack Books
is represented
by Inpress Ltd

Contents

Preface

Why did I get involved in the translation of poetry anthologies? The first time was during the Arab Spring, I wanted to share my floral spring and to echo the cry of liberty growing in the streets, so I worked on an anthology of female Arab poets, *Femmes poètes du monde arabe*, published by Le Temps des Cerises run by Francis Combes. The anthology was well-received by readers, several editions were needed, and artists and actors brought it to life. Then, I brought out an anthology of Syrian poetry, bringing together in particular love poems written 'in time of war and insurrection'. It was also due to my desire to open the frontiers of language to poets who suffer and live amongst destruction. After my book *Elle va nue la liberté* was published in 2013, I wasn't able to stand back from what was happening in the Arab world I came from.

I've always found translation a fascinating challenge. It's an exercise which resembles acrobatics, like high-wire walking: walking on a tight wire which moves between two worlds, two languages, two imaginations, two cultures. This need to translate, responds perhaps to need to be useful or to search to escape myself by serving others through poetry. Yes, translation is also a task of service, like being a mother, a cook, a bus, train or lorry driver. I out across thoughts and feelings. I allow people to be closer to one another, by opening the frontiers of language. Today, here is a collection of Kurdish female poetry.

I grew up in Lattaquié, a Syrian port. I don't recall if, as a child, there were Kurds in this town. And if there were any, I didn't understand what it meant to be a Kurd in Syria. During my studies in Damascus, I got to know young Kurdish men and women. My relationship with them didn't go beyond fraternal togetherness. We didn't engage in deep conversations. I knew nothing of their suffering; because all Syrians were suffering.

Syria was under the weight of silence and fear, news and relationships were controlled. Love affairs, friendships, work relations, everything was under control, listened in on. People said walls had ears.

The Kurds, for me, like the Druze, the Ismaelites, the Alawites, the Christians, the Sunnis, the Armenians, the Shiites, the Jews and the Circassians, are a thousand threads which weave together the beautiful human landscape of Syria. Their integrity and their rights must be equal.

In this anthology, which is a homage to femininity and to poetry of the highest order, forty-five female poets are gathered. They live in Syria, in Iraq, in Turkey, in Iran, in the autonomous regions recognised as such or fought over. The circumstances are not identical (for example, those of the Kurds were better in Iraq than in Syria, girls went to school and spoke their native language). Today, many live in exile.

Kurdish women are beautiful, poets, free spirits. They have often been described as combatant in uniform, carrying Kalashnikovs. I describe them as warriors with words. They belong to a people with a string oral tradition where poems are handed down from generation to generation, usually through song.

Today, they write and their poems travel by books, newspapers, the internet. They speak Kurmadji or Sorani. They write in one of two Kurdish languages, or in Arabic, Turkish, Persian even English or French. As Khonav Ayoub writes:

They put henna on their hair
Their hair is the path of
The old fatherland.
Love was threatened in their country.
They turned themselves into
warriors.

The right to speak their own language has often been denied. As has that of being baptised and addressed by their Kurdish names. One of the poets tells how she and her family, when she was a child, had to hide to light their candles on their birthdays.

I also discovered during this work that the Kurdish people

itself is a mosaic, with diverse beliefs. The Yazidi women, that Kurdish minority which practices one of the oldest religions in the world, have been a particular target for Daesh. When they came to their villages, they took them prisoner. They were abused and hellishly mistreated, being raped and seeing their families destroyed and tortured.

They are a patriarchal people, like all the people of the region, but the women play a major role, even in the political and military fields. They are a people too whose representatives have been killed on the streets of Paris, twice in ten years.

I wanted to convey my love and support by translating them and publishing them so they can be loved and admired. The other aspect I wanted to illuminate is that they are poets.

Being of Syrian origin, I imagine some, even amongst those closest to me will reproach me for encouraging or supporting Kurdish separatism. Therefore, I need to make my position clear. I think all people, all women, all men, all children should have the right to live in peace, freedom and dignity, to speak their language, to make their culture, their poetry, live.

I agree with the idea of recognising the right to cultural autonomy of all peoples. But it doesn't necessarily follow that national sentiment, however legitimate it may be, should result in the creation of new States. States and frontiers, today as yesterday, are often causes of war. The vital matter, in my view, is to cultivate understanding, mutual aid, even friendship between different peoples who share the same land. In fact, amongst all the peoples who share the same planet, whatever their history, culture or beliefs. Without racism, xenophobia, chauvinism. In a spirit of internationalism.

I edited this anthology to pay homage to Kurdish women. By taking part in the struggle of their people, they contributed greatly to the progress of ideas, towards democracy, equality between men and women. Witness the numerous women elected as mayors, working in partnership with men, and the feminist project they stand for.

But this book doesn't have a political aim. Above all, it's a book of poetry.

If I had the chance to speak more languages (apart from Arabic, French and English) I would embark on other projects of this kind in order to get to know poetry by women the world over.

As far as Kurds go, I was particularly motivated by the geographical closeness between me and them. The poems I've translated and adapted, and which are the majority of texts in this book, are from Arabic. I'm grateful to the friends who completed this selection with translations from languages I don't know.

I owe a debt also to Khonav Ayoub who helped me contact some of the poets, as I owe a debt to these poets who've put their confidence in me. I've never claimed to be a professional translator. For me, it's part of my idea of being a poet. I hope, in any case, I've been faithful to their poetry and that I've made their poems loved in a different language. And thank you for liking poetry and being curious about voices coming from afar.

Maram al-Masri

Kajal Ahmad

I don't want flowers

I don't want flowers
moments of union,
or dawns of separation.
I don't want flowers
because I am the most beautiful of flowers.

I don't want kisses
if to have them I have to
catch a prince
with a real dagger
no wedding day,
no dawns of divorce,
or twilight of widowhood.

I don't want a kiss
If through love, I become a martyr.
I don't want tears
on the coffin, where I am the corpse.

I don't want a cherry tree planting by my grave
out of sympathy
no flowers nor kisses,
no tears or lamentation.
Bring nothing. Offer nothing.

I die, a homeland without a flag, without a voice.
I'm grateful.
I want nothing.
I will accept nothing.

Amira Khaled Al-Abdiko

The White Hair Door

Oh, white hair

you who have taken
your whiteness
from the joyous clarity of my life

my joy that was held back by war
and bitten by the blackness of forced displacement
But
on which youthful roads
am I going to venture
to be as I ought...?

If you question the absent
about absence
will it return?

Because absence is a night and the return is the perfume
of a rose which smiles in the face of colours

And
if you question a sinner
will he repent what we
think of as a sin?

The stations of our lives drowned in
an old sadness
are only a moment
which has given wings to our days
so we can fly
into the space of a life
condemned by illusions

There is nothing on the horizon to bring a smile
because my youth has seen
many lost nights

Nothing can dissipate its blackness
except a silence full of tears.

But there will be a morning.

It will babble like a child

full of joy and music.

Sara Aktas

Return

Without a compass
Long ago we lost our women's direction
We've gathered losses in ourselves
We've burnt it with our toiling hands
It's a tornado which explodes beneath our skin

When the dawn becomes incandescent
What we kill by drinking poison
Is death
Don't think we will die
We are here
With our revolt which is hidden in the earth
With the severity of secret lakes
And with our hair in forty tresses

We come from the stupefying valley
We are women from an incandescent time
We have woken up from a loss
We lean against the mountain
With many sunsets in our eyes
We are reborn

The laments stick to our bodies
And between the sounds of percussion
We have torn the winding-sheet
Our cage has been broken
We have dissolved the magic of death
We have purified
And with our assembled hearts
And our silver virgins
And with our doves
We came with our infinite cries

We are the women of the lunar time
We were born in the silver night
We haven't forgotten the torment of massacres
And the wound of moonlight
We have lit a candle in the darkness

Loss faints in our hearts
We are reborn
With our ember faces

We have attenuated all the pain in our hearts
Our illuminated eyes brighten the darkness
We have left all distances in the arms of pain
Poleaxed
Scalded
We have understood our invisible chains
We have made a pact for the time of women

When Senem Hung Herself from the Paradise Tree

When Senem hung herself from the paradise tree
The sun didn't rise at the announcement of her death
So that her heart might grow cold again
If for a moment she had stopped
She should have seen the dawn before her eyes
An impatient goddess
And the eyes of her sister

Her chest crushed against the dawn wind
After the sun stopped rising
Grey clouds surround her
And solitude ran through the earth
When Senem hung herself from the paradise tree
She screwed up her eyes tightly
She stopped touching life
She closed her green eyes
'The groaning of the heart of this earth
The spirit of the times stands out,' she said

The fig leaf and the stolen apple
She remembered fairly-tales prisoners in the temple
She dived into the purity of feminine time
'Where I come from
I return to my femininity,' she said
History comes back to you

When Senem hung herself from the paradise tree
Her mother's long tresses
Attached themselves to the branches of paradise
Its white breasts cover her body
Its odour penetrates Senem
Her femininity began to cry
When Senem hung herself from the paradise tree
I would have liked to have been the tree.

Khonav Ayoub

Departure

Every day when you leave me
I close my heart's eyes
Set my fingers to the south
Me and my heart
We strain ourselves during your absence daily
My heart which is dead
How did you stay alive in him?

Only in your absence
I go from you to my pallor
Without you, I am here, silence of your absence
What would have happened
If you had restored the leftovers of our former separation?
Exile is another rock
Like your heart at the moment of farewell
Butterflies flutter towards you
No longer burning
You are now my living obscurity
Alone time leads away from me

Separation's morning is cold
My heart covers itself with your distant voice
Did you once dress yourself in a distant voice?
Your voice is my overcoat and my scarf

And my hand taps my shoulder
Like loss
In my street is a sweet-seller
Since you left
He sells sadness
And distributes the remains of oxygen

So we can let you live as much as us
Why can't we forget you?
You know nothing
Days have gone by in winter
Without rain
That town's lights aren't out
Night nor day, they've had enough
All have returned, without you,
They have decorated the Christmas-tree
With cotton because there's no snow.
But the tree didn't care.
What would it do with snow
And I alone will decorate this house
The neighbours' birds enter our house
They look at the sadness on the walls
And skedaddle as if they'd seen a wolf!
The sadness in your absence is a wolf
In your absence the door is torn off
And your absence is the door
I gave you a sign with the rain
So you raised farewell's umbrella
And you left as if you weren't there
As if I wasn't there.

The Kurd

The Kurd goes to war singing life
He comes back victorious
Then he sings for his friends
for those who didn't return
The Kurd never loses
He comes back a martyr or he doesn't return
He has never attacked anyone
He has always been a defender
And since when has defence been treason?
The Kurd is a prophet
Which is why all religions stab him
If they had left him his land
His song would reach the seventh country
If his enemy had understood his songs
then he would have sat down and cried for a thousand years
because he's a lover whose heart is burnt by absence
Even when he aims his rifle and puts
his finger on the trigger he thinks it's a
musical instrument, the 'saz'
Then he wants to play, he wants to live
But he surprises himself by the sound of
the dagger in his back.

Lara Ayoub

The absence of my love is bitter

The absence of my love is bitter
Don't try to satisfy me with a bouquet or a poem
When you arrive
We will be all and altogether satisfied
Me
My neighbour who is unhappy about my obsession with you
The florist I spoke to you about
My friend who never stops criticising your negligence
Your son who utters your name,
And my heart.
On I go with love,
And I wait for you, at your place, at our meeting place
And I'm going to speak of your ways to my town
So it will always remember you,
So that, when you arrive,
all its inhabitants will greet you

Set yourself on the riverbank
It will speak of you, even before you've   said a word
Then the taxi driver will take you to the Al-Hara café
where I waited for you so long.
The waitress will bring you a bitter coffee...
Because I've told her my love likes it like me
And the absence of my love is bitter.

***

Leave war a little
and let's listen to music
so we can enjoy life a bit
and so the saxophonist can play a little piece
that way their bullets can't reach us
We are going to live again
and death will stay far away
Come, so I can love you more
Come, because I love you more, now.

At the Beginning of November

I rush to the neighbouring café
Its walls are painted black
Its door is grey which lost its colour when it lost its beloved
The café owner is a woman of fifty
She offers us a cup of coffee and smiles
The cup bears the name Jean
Jean, her child, the one she brought into the world
after twenty-five years
Me too, I'm going to write about Jean
my child
the one I will love one day

      ***

Between love and politics
a homeland and a war
a rose which burns
endless treasons
urgent news about a lost lover
and red blood
between love and politics
O, my love
you
and me
and an murderous kiss

Ronak Aziz

A Tree Devoured by Fire

Peacefully I think of the distance between
      our last embrace and this eclipse
      bleeding in my heart
There are incommensurable and invisible spaces
Just like the pauses between a lover's
      kiss and a goodbye sigh
This frail mountain that you are, I fold it
in my shirt pocket,
What can be seen of it is
A little flower which is your tear.
Thinking peacefully of you and your ten fingers
that I ate on the day we met,
You said that that new fingers would grow
I am a man that God loves and he has given me his blessing
I contemplate all this white in your head
While you swim in a lake of crimson wine
Rainy women and a palpitating sea-coloured heart
And you are the distance between my tear and my smile
And between the law of attraction and the whole of this
      embrace
Even I am like that
Solitary, naked, like a tree consumed by fire

Embrace

The wrinkles I refolded in my pocket
The moment we met
I'm now on the *qui vive*, while starving birds
Eat my face
And I look for you
Only your first kiss knocks on my window from time to time.
I climb on a holy ziggurat.
I don't get to you.
I sing and I play with the fringes of my red skirt.
Every time I opened my eyes, I fell on you.

Wiam Badrakhan

Camp 1

I'm afraid the clothes pegs will stiffen
   while they are hung like
   me on the line, waiting for one of your
   items of clothing or a room where you set flying
   clouds of dust in the photo on my wall
I am afraid
Do you know how everything in me and around me
   is waiting for you with the impatience of the besieged
   for bread
Today, I'm writing another letter to you
   and I attach it like a nostalgic amulet to my chest
Write like me and attach letters
   from a distance on the washing line
I don't know how, but I think you will do it for me
Crises of nostalgia blow each winter
   and me I'm growing really old, mum
Crises of nostalgia blow while crying
   like the displaced before a green bus
   around me, under my pillow, on
   my plate, behind my windows, among
   the papers of my young students
   above my dislocated shoulder and in
   the middle of wounds which still bleed
Yes, I've aged and I don't even have time
   for a hiccup from my chest, so
   how not to write and you, how not to write?
There is no escape from the trap of the land,
   of the forest, without letters about these burns,
   mum...

Camp 2

We have known a camp in each town
        since our young childhood dreams, they
        told us it belonged to our brothers
And we heard of its thorns
        which prick every stranger who holds out
        their fingers in curiosity to open its
        windows
We arrived in the camps, become
        museums of a thickened memory
        of tribes surviving near the north of
        the ogre and his sons to the other ogre and
        his new sons
No one talks of thorns any more, but we
        begin to raise them, and polish them and
        we are becoming artists in the skill of
        pricking blindly those we
        called 'the camp's children'
Will a day arrive when delegations
        of the repatriated to visit our tents, to read a
        surah of the Koran and ask questions
        before our final condolences on the
        thresholds of oppression in our eyelids?
Will an entire generation deny
        us – we the late-comers – who can't
        file our nails as for ten years
        we have filed our anticipations and
        have grafted them with oppression's forms
And the beautiful ghosts will they be
        disgusted by what remains of the country of our
        narrow alleys, full of children and cats
who can't say hello in the morning
        in the languages of the countries from which
        they've returned, nor use a knife and fork

Will men let their children
      taste the pain in what
      the desire to live has been so
      maliciously hollowed out and left empty and
      not filled with alternative homelands?
We are familiar with a museum in each
      town and the day we were
      displaced, we carried away our museums
      and built camps and covered them
      with thorns
We are the 'children of thorns' not 'children of the camps'.

Kosert Ahmed Bakes

A Simple Sneeze and Life is Over

Don't go down the stairs
where you don't have a life...

Questions destroy the glory of the moon
And with a sneeze
They bring heaven to earth

In the evening, the bird fell
without leaving a trace Under
the monsters' feet
the bird will no longer know
it's nest...

The groaning of death's storm
is like the desert tornadoes It
awakens history's maledictions
puts its finger on the old
wounds and a new
episode revives its friendship
on earth

How long will this epidemic last?
it's war
my eyes are tanned
because of the walls' silence
I will declare suffering And
my tears

How can I know that my morning won't
contain only one anxiety My
feet rush in the alleyways My hands
hang onto a chest full of cries
And henceforth my heart beasts fast
lub-dub lub-dub
My fingers tremble
And a telephone dispenses the soul's buttons
With melodies
And life listens to all that
So a melody of the invisible
Withers it
A false smile
lub-dub lub-dub
Here I am, my heart beats faster then
it stops at the repair station
It takes off the oxygen mask
And life's chest fills
With the strange corona viruses
and my chest, my chest is
full of fire, Go up the stairs
the soul is yours
and if it comes to you from the other side
don't stay silent it's life
which belongs to you, No
don't stay silent
don't stay silent
No
no...

***

I'm tired
of following the traces of your love
Come back so I can take a bit of rest in your arms.
I've drowned in the rain showers of your growing cold
And all the same there are no floods
Give me your warm books
Because I'm out of breath
Take my hand
I don't want to become a happy fish
With a siren's imagination...
I am a grain of sand in History
Make me into your pearl necklace
I don't want to die
in the heart of some conch or other.

*

Nazand Begikhani

Your Look

Your look is a deserted path
It stretches towards a field
A cloud of letters takes flight
A profound anxiety
Between you and me

Your look is a line
Hung with words
It leans towards a latent form
A silent word
Between you and me

Your look is a smiling stone
It invites me to the dance
Beneath the wind's shadow
An oozing movement
Between you and me

Your look is a volcano
It carries to its burning summit
The union of two matters
The capsized bodies
Of you and me

Your look is a door
Open on a space
Full of tortures
A white sign carries us
Towards where? Towards what?

Love Passion

It's only in love the body becomes a leaf
And the head an enchanted violin
Your entirety
Is light shining!
You resemble Schubert's notes
And the wild space of Van Gogh
You are equal to a sublime sadness
To a deep depression
You are equal to a child's laughter
And my mother's burning tears
You are equal to all that moves
To all that flees
A harmonious but vertiginous movement
You are equal to a dancing feather
And like a deafening cry
You fly over all frontiers
The frontiers of isolation
And those of unity
The established frontiers of evil
And those of pleasure
You whirl like dervishes
You fly over frontier s of wisdom
And those of madness
You are no longer here or elsewhere
Oh! my likeness
Towards where do you turn
On the territory of absence?

Evening on the Loire

Alone
Like every afternoon
And old book under my arm
I walk by the side of the Loire

And I hear them say
It's a time of drought
The Loire no longer tintinnabulates
And no longer offers her silky flowers
To the wind's loving hands

And the Loire is the silhouette of a wounded season
Passing sweetly

Here is a group of coloured children
Skimming sweet flat stones across the face of the Loire
Their orbs' sudden eddies
Are the looks of old decayed women
Sitting in the day's emptiness
And dreaming in the morning of time

And the Loire is a fine line
Stretching towards a grey valley

And there are drunken men
Brushing from their shoulders
The violet dust of the years
And their empty bottle
Are the golden harnesses of their loneliness

And the Loire is the sweet note of a flute
Rolling peacefully
And they are happy to say
It's a time of drought
And the sea's halcyons don't dance
And the rocks no longer dream
And the Loire is an eagle with broken wings
Passing quietly

And I hear them say
It's a time of drought
The deep blue look of the Loire
An exiled poet
Walking with an old book under her arm
Saying good evening to the Loire
And disappearing

Leyla Mexo Berazî

The Chestnut Girls

He breaks with a stone the *fanu* we are
The former mines which surge shine to right and left
They have taken our names which they didn't like
In their pockets the stamp of a history
On today's sheet and in their alphabet
They show sang-froid and annoyance
Behind us, to our left, this autumn
For that one, for the dead one are born the chestnut girls
Very late, close by, narcissi blossom

Serenity of the Flowers

You close your green eyes and you left
For the memory of my brother Mehmet Atas

We get ready for a golden summer
With the little sounds of squirrels
This way, water flows with courage
Beneath the fresh shadows the flowers grow
For your heart
In nature's womb
On a tribal pelisse
We were worthy as a ray Year
After year, they fell

From the sky, above a little town in
A place apart, the stars fall towards the bottom
The god was in a cold solitude
He took his vengeance with anger against us

Yara Biran

Each time I stood before

Each time I stood before
a movie camera I kept my mouth shut
I was afraid of laughing
or perhaps I was ashamed
of my big front teeth
which hid behind them
my sadness and my joy
behind them for a long time inside me
the sound of the agitation of joy
My big eyes made me more
confident they which carried
rivers of elegant sadness
overflowing each time from woman's coffin
on its way to our town's cemetery
rich in dead
A woman who has forgotten her meal over low heat
like my mother
leaving mouths behind her
The variegated hunger pursued them always
As long as they lived under
their chains
They had a light similar to Spring
which hesitates to arrive
Behind my thick lashes
very thick
I've carefully hidden your photo
to spread dew on my heart
to resist drought and thirst
And sometimes to wipe away
the saltiness
and the mist of tears

my soul's mirror
Leaving to my cracked lips
another chance
to smile without fear
of the
same joy

*

Your old photos are so warm
In black and white
How do you know it...
How much white plunging into the soul's
cellars to enlighten

*

Like a blind person who has lost their sight
But who has kept the soul's clarity
my heart
follows your traces

*

Like a predatory wolf
Soon aged
I hear its howl
In my chest
Until dawn
This brawler's heart

Sîmîn Caycî

Woman Life Liberty

Women have become a symbol of life
Their hair is liberty's banner
They have cried
'I don't want a life of modesty
And slavery'
Well done girls!
The children of the revolution and water
have become the leaders of the revolution
In a sunny country
A homeland become One as its aim
They shouted at the tops of their voices.

'Woman Life Liberty'
Has become the world's banner

Once more the sense of revolution
has given a soul to the street
The kiss of the wind dancing
on the girls' fringes
in the smell of gunpowder and smoke
tight bands
of cries in the night
against the enemy of time
People hand in hand
All with one voice

'Woman Life Liberty'
It's become the world's banner

The revolution coloured
In blood
will never stop
Thousands of magnificent audacious girls
have sacrificed their life for that
It's how the tree of liberty
grows with blood
The day of vengeance is not far away
The reign of the enemy will disappear
A homeland become One through struggle
They have all shouted at the tops of their voices.

'Woman Life Liberty'
has become the world's banner.

Town

These days, I detest
everything
about me which is no longer me
about you which is no longer you

The hatred in my soul eats
cinders
It eats me and rises in my red veins
I don't know what fire devours me today

When the town goes mad
I become, me, mad for you
madness in my head
Justly mad
The mad can deceive and laugh with laughing
gaze so as not to shed tears

Alleys full of painful maledictions
A street beneath our black
And red feet
A girl who can't catch you
Fariyad Fariyad
Fariyad
Who is fire consuming today?

Majda Dari

Poet

Up to now,
I haven't thought myself a poet
It convinces me that to wash the dishes
lights up the shadows of night
and purifies dust and boredom
and me I feel anxious
like every woman
who is afraid to sing in her solitude
It makes me quiet with a kiss
so that we are transformed
into tender music and a glass of wine.

The Narrow Emptiness

Your hands pour your blood into my glass
There is no more room for another emptiness
I've closed the transparent curtain of the heart
Every night a new episode of cold
The talisman is scattered in all astonishment's directions
I block the bleeding hole
obscurity fills the places
and presages the end
I explain it playing with the moment
the wounds of pain under my skin
tires my heels
I leave quietly
A town inhabited by gelatinous beings
and a great slowness
The circus grows larger
and a great atrocious emptiness falls into the depths
my fleeing respiration increases
a man of fire cuts the grey shadow
the air scatters in the little rooms
I gather a small tear in the mirror's corner
carrier who can't carry soul
I pretend to smile at the loss with
A bit of blood on my lower lip
It's enough to pour the emptiness in the emptiness
I no longer have room to receive any more
the whiplash of your absences
in life's brouhaha.

I Will Raise Stars to Illuminate Your Next Winter

I imprison the air in time's corridor
I bury songs in the corners of the house
I turn the eye of night
And in my most powerful lack of you
I offer you wine in the jug of my hands
I bolt the river and I lose the key in the fissures of water
All the doors of the wishes in my eyes
What else
A cup of dawn juice
Spreading the perfume of my dress scattered in the corners
To remove anxiety's dust
I laugh in haste
And try remorse
Can I recover from my sick memory?
I recount the violin on your fingers
Each night is a butterfly
Much rain
Winter is the heart's passion
And the orange is a quarter stuck
in a woman's hair
who cooks ice for a salted wound in
your chest
The habits of absence hurt me
They come once and burn all
Meanings.

Sarwin Darwish

One day I will have

One day I will have
Two wings of palm
Trees who said that I
couldn't leave?

In my heart are numerous prophecies
My heart says you come
Carrying our mad heart
To crown me on the throne of
                    perfection
This long and hard journey
is going to pass which you call life
And I will live in epochs
Where the homeland wasn't in ashes

And I will live in places
Where there are no wars or destruction
Where the sun shines in your eyes

One day I will have
Two wings of palm leaves
Then...
Who said I couldn't leave?

*

Someone waits for me so I can be
his shadow
And there are those who view me badly
so I can live
and speak and get dressed and

think I cry like
him
I change into a cry
Into noise
Into paint brushes of colours
To transform my reality as
a human being
The colours which drip on me
never point to joy
My voice shelters the groaning of the flute
And the laughter of a girl who has never been a girl.

Avin Kissra Mahmoud (Dibo)

Hold out the palm of your hand

Hold out the palm of your hand
so I can embrace
God's face
And so you can keep what he has granted you
Because I have no desire to be
an atheist
Caress my head with your verses
and listen to his hymns
From the first matter trembling

The devil coughs
I'm here
as if we don't know who you are
and who created you,
Don't wake us up from prostration
For our ablutions would be wasted
And we would perish.

*

When I searched for myself
I found myself in the places I dread the most
With you!

Don't touch my heart
forgetting your finger prints upon it
so the world won't accuse you
of the blackness which occupies it

I thought it was an embrace
I didn't know
I was going to die

It happens you include all your capital of lies
in a single response
'I'm fine'
When all the strangers around you
ask
How are you?
I had to abandon myself to you
on your shoulders
to take a rest
And to shout about what was in my heart
Even if the world after that must face up to
resurrection

*

Do you know what it means that the sun
rises in the East?
It's your absence
Some traits are truces in life and
a few voices are breaths in the soul
Stab me in the heart
because there is no longer
a place in my back for
the dagger
I don't believe in joy
I always beg for my sadness
I don't have as much fear of death
As of love
The fist has no need of a living body
and the second needs a thousand bodies living
in you
For every soul, there is a window
If you close it well again you will suffocate
Beginnings are always pretty
but ends are our most beautiful
beginnings

Tarifa Dusky

To a Mad Writer

1
A savage revolution... You are!
Only the revolution becomes
a wave,
Only the revolution can become these lines
Which surround us
Only the revolution can transform my poem into rain
Refresh the drought of your entrails!
But the sea too
Like you... mad!

You couldn't read me, feel
my femininity
you couldn't read me,
sense my mauve gardens!
You couldn't dissimulate
love's revolution
in your cigarette's smoke!
You couldn't see the love
growing within me!
You couldn't resist your body's fire,
You can't renounce your desires
That's why you relax
every day among pomegranates
in luxuriant gardens!
To change you into a king,
a husband
a revolutionary!
Then you came back to look at the window
Looking for the fire
which transforms your

snow into sparks,
which will fall on your head!
Madman.
I can't describe you to others!
It makes no difference to you
Between
She... me... other women!
You give yourself up to lust without fire

2
I made an illogical decision
when I left you
I don't complain about your remoteness
My heart blames me

My father
Between me and him, a love story
of a different kind
I cling to his smell
His love won't come again
He's my father
Your given name
Your name floats above me soul
I'm going
to chase it away

Love has no weight
But it has worn me out
it's broken the back of my words

Elham Erfan

The trees tremble under the bastard brambles

The trees tremble under the bastard brambles born of the axe
Our garden henceforth is without scent and of the oranges
nothing remains but the bitterness of chagrin.
From this chagrin, let love flow, from the bitterness
which tightens the throat, swallow your tears.
This time, it's the remains of your chagrin which
       appears to you like the noble dregs of an old wine.
These seducers without virtue are worse than the Devil;
even God is astonished by
       the go-getting of these upstarts.
In this bazaar, it's the rule pf profit for the impostors.
Branding with red fire the heads of the shoe-makers
the humble, is already planned by them.
Proclaim and announce your path.
Traveller!... How long are you going to stay silent?
Go to the limit this time, because your cry is the ultimate way.
Go! Renew tradition; knock on the door as in the time of
Spring, in the past; because winter is a demanding,
Hypocritical visitor, henceforth forever the interloper.
Love! Even if you have hurt yourself as night passed, marker
by seas, light a lamp, because that is what triumphs in the end.

*

This earth is pregnant with an in-commen-sur-able revolt, like
an apple girded by the hands an in-comm-en-sur-able Devil.

Ah! Brother Joseph, the youngest son of
the prophet Jacob, is prey to wolves,
since the word has transformed itself into
Canaan, into an in-comm-en-sur-able pit.

An anger, a wrath, stifled, will remain forever
a cry drowned in chagrin;

Freedom is dispersed, disappeared; in-comm-en-sur-able
has become the prison.

For an in-comm-en-sur-able storm the sea is getting itself
ready, the sea which drowns tears.

From the enclosure, the castle wall will never know
           that brick by brick, will it will arrive at the
           end of its race and the in-comm-en-sur-able
           full stop.

Get up, so as not to stay alone and lost at the end of the road,
because, no doubt, beyond this dead end, there will be an in-
comm-en-sur-able way.

Let the father land plunge into the sun's rays as they are life's
treasure and deserve an infinite protector.

Roonak Faradji

I love you with half my heart

I love you with half my heart
With the other half I kiss the beautiful
        street children

I kiss you with half my lips
And with the other half I call the names of
        This town's women

I flirt with you with half my body
And I carry toolbars with the other
        half

I watch you with one eye
And I watch the mountains of our land
        with the other

I caress you with one hand
And I caress the wounds of the street with
        the other

Half my head is on your shoulders
And the other half is buried on the shoulders
        of the people.

Mizgin Hasko

The Earth's Angels

Formerly
I used to think angels inhabited the heavens
There where paradise
is close to the divine throne
with riverbanks surrounded by vines
which give off the scent of flowers
But now I see
them here among us
always ready to support our patients
without fear
or panic
with hearts full of love
Invisible tears wept
They pray for life every moment
between dangerous waves
They are the angels,
the lights of God...
Leave him!
Leave God in his realm
No longer call him by his names
Call him what you like
And now turn towards our world.
They are angels
The same angels
Candles in the dark
Candelabras in the dark seas of despair
They guide us
On the path!

Maha Hassan

All the Village Came Together Here

Everybody came, the old folk the girls, the young men. It was
 like going out for a big picnic, a group picnic. The women
 brought food and drink so the family wouldn't spend a lot
 of time arguing. As if they were at a wedding, the wore
 fine, fresh-smelling clothes for this great get-together
 when no one stayed at home but everybody came.

There were those who asked for her to be killed in public:
 'Kill the bitch.' Voices were raised
Everyone came together in the centre of the village, on the big
 square:
'Kill her. She ruins our children's minds, entices them to
 immorality. Her poems betray their minds and corrupt
 their thoughts.'

'Don't we have a way of defending our ideas other than
 killing? Why are we killing those who are different
 from us. It's a different mentality, and another culture,
 we must listen to her and draw the lessons, not kill her.'

'Why kill her, let her write, and when words put
 people's lives in danger.'

'Kick her out. Throw her out of the village. It won't do any
 good to kill her. You'll make her a symbol, and her obscene
 poems will gain an audience greater than before.'

'He must kill her to prove he doesn't think like her.'

Opinions diverge and the debate has gone on for a long time
between those who want to kill her and those who want to
expel him, between those who asked for a withdrawal and
those who demanded his expulsion.

And as the scene was replayed, the other loses, the individual
and the group gains.

The vote for her murder was above 80%.
The others were against the decision to kill her,
but in favour of her exile.

And as no one knows her family and because she had no
relatives, no brother, father or cousin who could kill her,
the village decided to choose ten men to get together
to do it, one by one, and the one who gave the
fatal blow would be called the village's hero and
he would be given a medal.

Before the first ten approached her... like a butterfly,
Amira the poetess got up and flew away

She fled to the desert, the red desert which previously was
green. Everyone has chased her, the ten men and the
rest of the population. The old men the young,
the children, the women and the men, all running across
the desert

'She's a witch, a fairy... It's the proof the proof. Kill her!'

'She's sacred... Don't touch her.'

Opinions diverged again.

In front of everyone. Amira slowly undressed. She stood
naked before the astonished faces, she sang her poems
in a warm, touching tender voice as if a genie or a
fairy were dictating her words or melodies.

'Go girls... Forward, girls... O girls of freedom... Join me...
Come and comb my hair... come and bathe here
daughters of Aphrodite, Eve and Venus.

Suddenly savage nature was transformed into a paradise...
a green paradise.

The sirens are there... the girls are
totally naked... they swim in the water which springs
from a magic place, secret and invisible, the earth on
which they stand is transformed into a spring of
clear water, suddenly filled with coloured roses

The men dropped their knives and their killing tools,
astonished.

And heavy rains fell...

White, transparent rain...

lustral...

pure...

refreshing...

The red washed... the red desert shone with colours and the
green shone. The green grass, tender and the new dew-fall.
A cosmic spring was created at that moment jets of
water sprang forth here and there, embraced, exchanged
kisses... and slept

The women swore, sighing with love, lying under the men,
they saw the faces of Sultana and Rehana drawn in
the sky, laughing.

Fatema Hersan

Whistling

I close my eyelids
On my grandmother's drawn curtains
And the roses on her garden
And some of her thorns stuck
In the carnations'
Memories
And the Damas rose buds
I fall asleep in the foam of this dream
I visit the alleys
I kiss absence
And the dead
I forgot a little of myself over there
And with a half-wink of joy
I gathered the fleeing mirrors
I have firmly closed the pits
So they can't tell stories
I've cut the grass's borders
And deafened a murmur's suffering
I fold the curtains
Of habit
I proclaim distance's borders
No fear blocks the horizon
I hold out my hands to the light
And I make the whistling stop.

A Skylight in the Heart

My breath is short
And getting rapid
The doctor has made me realize
that my heart was lazy
It was hit by many bullets
Which have formed a hole the size
of a bird
since that day every hunter falls from it
without me wanting him to

A Stubborn Apple

I need an inventory of my disappointments
And I share timidity's clouds
I shake my voice
I pull stronger ropes
I pour gunshots from above and kill
At the height of joy
I ignore the mirror before me
I am inhabited by nothingness
Sometimes I lose my voice
my heart trembles like
a stubborn apple
refusing to fall
in spite of all the frost.

At the Lights

At the traffic lights the rain
Hits the glass of my heart
in a rhythm of peace with death
It ravishes the drowsy moment
Of two lovers
as they whisper with their lips
And off I go in silence
Ignoring them
My heart's beating
announces their racket
And the link to this scene
has hit the silence like a thunderbolt

A Pile of Nails

I claim to be strong
Scrape the rust of my joints
No vibration nor breakdown My voice
Vibrates in the echo And my body rivals
The emptiness
The day delivers its deposits
I launch myself like fragile
      firewood
Silence inhabits me
The bones of my neck make war on me like
the leaves with which I hide my heart
The famished plate of my vocabulary
      looks at me fixedly
It provokes my coldness And
it is sure
that all this powerful fleet is only
a handful of nails

Bahar Hossein

They will never be closed

They will never be closed
my soul's
little windows
they will stay open and luminous
in spite of the destruction
of thousands of wishes and hopes
so as not to block the route to thousands of aims
and new aspirations

Poem

I destroy my memories
to say to the street full of dust
which once you removed from my sight
that I'm in your place now
Look
the moon is on the road
You can raise your palms towards your face
and keep your head straight
I swear, by the time of despair and ingratitude
that I've seen traces of steps in the mud
become drunkenness and comfort

I used to be
like the grass in the pond's mud
like a tree trunk
at the edge of a bridge
until you arrive, like the sun
softly, softly.
You have become my footsteps
I'm no longer a relaxed sea which awaited
        sleeping waves
nor a little caterpillar too tired
to become a butterfly

Now
I'm the union of the heart and the road
the spirit and echo of a corpse's breath
full of life's movements
they are all the reason for this position taken
in the face of a stifled cry
which have taught me I'm your shadow
my pine
O my adored pine

Rehab Fawaz Hussein

Handfuls

Dreams tame me
With handfuls of illusion
I look
like a sterile tree
which gives birth only to
wishes
Only the mirror
Sustains me
witness to my femininity's
greyness
like love's widow
who curses
the whiteness
casting childhood in the womb
of tragedy...
She carries her heart
between her palms
It slides generating chaos
debris
And those eyes
shining with hope
have slipped into obscurity
And the last thread of
the sunset
has been cut
The clouds have searched for
the hail of panic
And have drowned the vague terrains
of tears...
The soul's nudity is the most severe
the most painful
of the body's clothes

Even Ibrahim

Letter to a Friend

I chew the white flower my child has hidden between her
      green eyes waking from a nightmare
I chew a little white rose she
      hid for me in her short hair
Which sometimes make me
Afraid to look at her
I chew and sing
You are very beautiful
But my heart is broken
You are alone like me
But the sad trees by the road need a friend
I chew a white flower and sing
There is no love in this house
What would I chew if my little girl left one day
If she no longer came back from her nightmare
I chew a white flower
I think about a svelte woman who loves red and hats
A sweet woman who hides her sadness in roses and rings
Who approaches love without a heart
I chew a white rose
I have put the other in the long hair of the night
I look for a green ghost which looks like your tender fingers
Which would give me back my faith in love and I don't find it
My neighbour has told me that the fig tree in my back garden
      is full of fruit
She's also said she was supervising my back from the window
      which looks out onto my kitchen
And she feels a strange joy when she sees me dance at three
      o'clock in the morning with half-naked demons
She said she couldn't believe that I'm the same woman who

wears new glasses and won't open the door to a
      stranger
I look for a white rose to put in your hair
A little rose says to the universe that women who look strong
      and bright on this page are the same who lose
      themselves at the end of the night between black
      and white,
Ronak,
A woman doesn't look for love after her first
She tries all the time to find a pot to fill all this space
She follows happiness which has been lost on the path of love
She looks for a new candle to light the evening
Regarding a book which tells what she didn't know
      about herself
Regarding a cup of mint tea which waters her soul's tree
For something that hides her beauty
She hides her excessive tenderness and her tears
      which fall without reason
For her life's lost time.
Time is in your hands and now, Ronak, and you fear leaving
I chew a white rose and think
One day
One day
Your eyes in the photo won't be sad
You will stand behind the man who loves you
Your trembling hand
strangles the angel
on its shoulder your fragile fingers
come together gently to make a hole in its back
Standing behind the man who loved me
You put your fingers in his back
You touch my heart for once
To think that they all watch both of us
We are two broken women that
time has transformed into two eccentric cats
Love has given them everything to worry about
You are afraid

You hurt others without knowing
I'm afraid too
Sometimes I hold on with one hand to understand others
Your eyes won't be sad this evening in the photo
You know how doors change places
You give this man what he wants
in the bathroom
behind your heart's thick wall
in the corner of this cracked mirror
You will suddenly discover
the reason for the tears which assault you in bed
The mirror won't give you what you want
Your eyes will look dead in the photo standing
behind a man who has never loved a woman
the man no one sees except me
And you in the photo,
Ronak,
do you like the white roses like me.

Vian Juma

If I was a prophet

If I was a prophet and I'd met God
I would have begged him,
I would have kneeled at his feet
and would have asked him
to send his soldiers
to save the earth
I would have cried and begged
Near to his altar with a burning chagrin like a mother who ties
        a single shoe for her only son
I would have kissed the throne's borders
on which he was seated
And I would have begged him singing
to have pity on a people
on a nation which has experienced the worst
and which continues to suffer
and to taste the venom of death
beneath the lash of justice

I would say to him that
The orphans' field is the greenest of the corn fields
And that the tears of the bereaved are more numerous
than the ants of the earth
And that the widows are more numerous
than the trees and that
mourning has become the colour of Iraq
And that blood has become the official drink
of this poor people
If
I was a prophet

I would have ordered my angels to alter life's scales
        and to transform
men by fatwas into poets
and politicians into composers and singers
and the weapons of mass destruction
into musical instruments
So the children of martyrs can play them
I would have transformed the battlefields
into fields for butterflies and squirrels
and the parks
into lovers' meeting places so that lovers can kiss there
I would have transformed
Daesh into a sugar doll
And the
war planes into wandering dreams
which offer rapid wishes
I would have imprisoned Arzrael
in the middle of the bottomless sea
And stacked up all its cruel past in
a sealed bottle
then I would have
thrown it out of the universe.

Xunav Kano

Black Feather

During the war
I ran towards you
To save what is left of me
I put my head on your shoulder
to sleep forgetting the blood's disorder
And the cold that falls asleep
to wake in me a tender
night.
The night
I came to you tired out
The sofa groaned with love
All the books on the shelves
saw me
Something in me... sees you
But doesn't look at you...
Death has dispersed me
Black dove, I was
Each of my feathers
falling on a grave.
My eyes were there to see it
And my poetry
to attract your attention
a place for us to meet
Today, nothing
Only my tears and my solitude...
I won't give birth to a new heart
I am a dried out tree
Everything in me is withering
I have never been a ring
slipped onto the finger of Fate
You were the destiny

that broke my fingers
All the pearls of sweat
shine on my forehead
without you arriving
Under the tree, there was earth
Before I fell on my heart
All the mirrors lead to shadows
The windows are open
Hope has flown
and the wind has entered
We didn't go to the sea
so I might return parched
The signs are all green
But my heart is black...
These tears
they rain every day
I don't wash my face in the morning
I walk
Each step is a tear
All along the path
eyes leave their orbits
I am a butterfly
without wings
A stone on the road
The passers-by don't move it
Does a candle burn
and shed no light?
Where do the bodies lie?
The earth turns
Do the coffin's lids move?
This rose
which grows in me
will remain dumb
O you, all the waves
You won't be able
to crumble it into sand
The pain won't go away.

The Country's Saleswoman

I think
How did you bring me into the world?
you and my father?
And how
did the martyrs' fathers and mothers
give birth to their children?
How did you give birth to me?
I'm ashamed of my mind's complexes
Oh mother
All the faces I met
had their eyes fixed
on my chest
and their hands were wrapped round my waist
Isn't there a man in this world who
loves me?
My mother,
unhappiness to this body.
Let my nipples fall
like autumn leaves.
Let the devil take my vile lips.
Let them be buried!
My mother
Why has the whole of humanity abandoned its humanity
and why does it stare at my vagina?
Humanity
looking for a senseless warmth
like the lips of starving men
Do male martyrs also think
Of my body before going to sleep?
All the men I've encountered
have kissed my virginity as if I was their mother 'Kurdistan'
The developers of pre-Islamic culture
ate chickens whole.
They left us only the bones.

Let me be a rope
so poets and creatives can play with...
To protect the descendants of our culture
My mother
and to give birth to poems
by men of my tribe.
My mother,
all the men
were kissing me
like they were kissing the letters of our alphabet
And they search my breasts for
drops of milk so sweet
before it can be spoiled by blood
They all
Caressed the forest of my head...
They are tents God deployed
on our identity
My mother
Every morning I replay a
Nocturnal scene
The era: my long life...
The place: a chest where I look for a fatherland
I swear by my fatherland
My mother
that my dream
my ultimate dream
is
one evening...
a rose...
a quick kiss
and a fatherland.

Rogen Kedo

No One Like Me

I have worked like a man in a factory
like a female farm worker in the fields
a building worker
milkmaid and shepherdess of a flock of
sheep a gardener in my father's garden
caretaker of the paternal home during the war
a musician
and a silent participant in demonstrations
I have been everything
before becoming a migrant
Now, everything is available
for me here
except the fatherland
and the smell of my father
and mother.

Fadwa Kilani

I haven't pulled this place with me

I haven't pulled this place with me
this far
The name is the same
The two dates overlap
The dates all overlap
My balcony looked out on this place
As on a sea
But it's different from today's balcony
The dirt has a different smell the two
Chairs the table the coffee itself
The same
cups
The pictures themselves hung
Everything is similar
and different
We are there both of us
We are both
Here

....

There is a space-time
shortened by ardour
A space of time
we have rolled behind us
It came with us onto the aeroplane...
It sat
with us on the chair
It came down with us... it is strange too
We pile it up now in this café

Here the sea is different
There is another sea
the coffee itself
has a different taste
The wrinkles have creased our faces
And there
is what hasn't changed like the
conversation we carry on,
our laughter goes on,
the cup which tips over, as usual,
on what we have written.
Before going back once more
let's remember the distance between this far
place
...and this place

The frost's thread grows longer
now in the distance
So everyone dreamt of it
there are no towns
no summits no joy.

If I can, one day, I will return
to the peace of the kidnapped fatherland's
and I will drive away the flies which land
on its wounds.

Dunea Al Marchawi

Letters dampened by tears and a heart full of noise

They know nothing today of yesterday...
Feelings pitch
and strengthen their never spoken secrets
a thousand stories and a tale the butterflies
send flying into the field of the age
Now they have a strange paralysis
Who are they singing for?
Their town's gardens are flattened
and happiness left the sky
long ago
Night has made her black dress fall on itself
They no longer smile
Only warm tears, a feeling
of nostalgia and a memory which will never return
Everything is outdated
And names and things have left
The flute is in mourning.

I am covered in wounds
All my limbs bleed
In my heart there is a pain
that no one-else can comprehend
The cry of silence wounds and wounds
And is nothing more than a sound
even if I cry harder

So
Bring the absent back to me
And on this sad day
Your shadow always haunts my heart
To what
Extent is this memory painful?
My eyes cry blood
Oh dear Sinjar
Oh my God, tormented, homeless, a martyr.
How is the maleficent beast to die?
And how to live in peace
I want to remove your wounds and worries
I want to fall asleep with you
Above your earth, your plain and your mountains in
harmony.
Ah, Sinjar
The figs will grow again
And hope will rise with the breeze
And everyone will return and you will rise up of course
said to me the sun
and the morning's birds

Bejan Matur

Ceremonial Robes

In the cold and devastated heart
Of these lands
I saw with my own eyes
Everyone was there with their voices
and their attitudes
We know someone best when we make love,
when we corrode our hearts together.
Growing heavier, our body
wakes us at night
The houses with yards are like tombs
Childhood is a sleep, a desire to touch
A breath which goes on and on
a desire which pulls us towards death.
I tested myself in each body,
I abandoned myself in each town.
I took the country's sky into my heart
and when I saw the emptiness in my heart
I said, it's time to leave.

Inside the shaping ceremonial robes
the roots are balanced on coat hangers
even if we throw fire into the sea
it will burn forever,
it burns a gift of desolation to obscurity
Perhaps history is a mistake, says the poet
humanity is a mistake, says God
Much later
in a future corrupted like the earth's heart
humanity is an error, says God
I'm here to correct it
but too late

The wave of red water without life,
the road follows night,
the poor earth peppered with travellers,
the white winding-sheets which balance,
ceremonial robes
The one thing necessary for a race
is the horse's mane.
It's the truth,
now we are here rotting
in a rut

God must not see the letters of my screenplay
Humanity is a mistake, he repeats.
And to correct his mistake
he gives grief,
only grief

*

The children's tombs

So we are dead.
We have escaped the shadows.
The hedges saw us
and the tiny stones.

Night and stars have passed over us.
We have been buried on the roadside.

Night Spent in a Patient God's Temple

I
You have chosen your exile amongst the mountains
  swept by rain.

Where you hung back last night
Was the patient god's house
The house where a human is endowed with compassion.
No need for temples, I say.
This is simply a place.
The human soul must surely be a temple.
And let the river of homeless rain
Remind us of God and childhood.

II
You chose your exile amongst the mountains swept by rain.
The beauty of committing mistakes
And peace and pain.
Everything leads you to the void
And you, you looked at patience's pale flowers and you cried
You slept in his arms as if nothing existed
There will be a journey towards the mountain
and chosen exile
And a human chosen by God

We must listen once more to this music
The place wasn't made for loving

The Earth's Dream

In its solitude the night sky thought,
Why these stars?
Why this voice which hums in my tenebrous heart?
When the voices move away
What is left?
Only the oppression which gnaws my soul.
If the pole star leaves its place for a second
Will the fisherman lose his way?
Will the shepherd lose his whistle?
Perhaps nothing,
nothing, can change my truth
I am the earth's dream.
A sleeper finishing his sleep
will see when he wakes the true
obscurity of the beyond.

Widad Nabi

Don't Explain to Anyone

Why do you leave when you should stay?
Why do you laugh when you should stay silent?
Why are you silent when you should speak?
Why the bags under your eyes?
Why do you stop writing?
Why do you turn your back on your friends and on life too?
Don't explain anything to anyone
Why do you put your heart out to dry
like a piece of meat for fast-days?
Why do you poke out your eye
            with the finger of the one you love?
Why do you throw the memory of your body in the sea
            for the carnivorous fish?
Why do you often fall from the open wound of life?
Why do you forget your keys outside the door?
Why do you prefer to walk barefoot when you have shoes?
Why have you stopped complaining and questioning
yourself?
Why do you own everything and aren't happy?
Don't explain to anyone
Something whose reasons you don't know
Because, when you left your country, with a little backpack
You left behind you, there, all the answers.

A Place Lit Up by Memory

*for the houses we abandoned during the destruction, absence
and bombardment.*

Pain is
Visiting the ruins of our house in a dream
And you come back without its dust
       sticking to your hands

*

Tenderness
Is to water faded flowers
In your neighbour's garden
Because your house's flowers have
       dried out during bombardment

*

Distance
is pain's geography
Between two towns separated by thousands of kilometres
The first, is the one where you left your clothes on the line
the second, is the one where you hold out your hand
to retrieve your clothes from the first-floor balcony

*

Your hand stuck on the old house's bell which tells you
'Houses aren't for those who have left.'

*

Only the water
knows why flowers cry
on the balconies of happy homes
those we have left

*

On the way to your new house
There is a long nostalgic path
You will no longer walk

*

If you touch the hard metal of the moving bus
A daffodil will grow there on your iron door knob
This is how houses honour their exiled owners

*

You wake up every night in the middle of sleep
The tap is still pouring in your former kitchen

*

Life wouldn't be so bad
It would give you a new house
But your soul will remain a wolf
Howling every night
On the steps of your old house

*

Behind your old window
Your photo watches the rain falling
The hedge cries
And no one notices

*

The darkness
Pushing into abandoned houses
like April grass
however, the place
is lit up by memories

After the War

1.
The country which gave us our sad names anxious mothers
and a national hymn which glorifies killers
after a quarter of a century and a war
will it grant our coffins
the right of entry?

2.
After the war
we will forget all this pain
and we will smile amongst the ruins
crying

Narin Omar

Mirror and Book

As I love the mirror and the book
In the mirror I see you
Every morning
It says what I would like to say to you by demasking me
The book
I close me eyes on your photo
Every evening
A few moments before going to bed.

The Martyr Burns

The martyr:
Oh mother, I was afraid of the underground fire
So I sacrificed my soul
For those who are the earth's surface
And in my blood, to water the earth
Let the trees grow like the promised gardens of Eden

The mother:
Oh son, I've hooted after you
And I danced around your body
To be one of these mothers who have
Paradise beneath their feet!

The martyr:
Oh, me...
The flame burns me my mother!

The mother:
How my heart burns at the moment of separation
Of your soul from your body

Koestan Omarzedeh

A Woman in the Revolution's Flames

Listen to the odour of freedom
on the barrel of the gun
The revolution has broken out
has shone
and the country
has changed
into a single colour
And
We just
hear
Zina's voice!
It's the dance in silken hands
it's her
it's vengeance's cry!
This country
sings the song of freedom!

Is it a dream
or an autumn butterfly
which cuts injustice's fingers?

The revolution's flame arrives
and confronts this season.
We are going to break it,
the town's silence

I am a creative girl
Whose eyes are open
full of imagination and freedom
Come
and spread the flame of this revolution
Display it
In your hair

The North wind of freedom
and autumn's smile
have made it rain
on the ears of corn
in the mountains
and on the villages of this country

Everyone hold the torch
Everyone get up

In autumn
the rose of spring
has flowered decorating
with red
the fatherland's neck
so you can yourselves become citizens

So we are going to reach the flame of this revolution

Until the
uprising!

Sarwah Osman Mustafa

To My Friend

To my friend
Hey, my friend
To you all the dances
All the inspirations...
And the adoration...
I disperse my leaves...
And I poured myself, love's rain
Overflowing with passion
Hey, you the god of this existence
You are the road's compassion

My soul is opened up
And from my rays
I have woven golden threads
Hoping that I will illuminate
The path for millions of people
Now, it's enough...
Enough, to remain seated
Enough, of prison.
The time
Has come
For laughter...
For dancing...
For adoration...
In all innocence and sincerity

O lover

You still don't know
that time has passed
And the years pass one after another

And fingers still play on the strings
For a heart which won't sound
The ills won't intimidate it, nor groans,
To play on a heart is
Like playing the oud and to toying with the heart,
When it sings the song of love
It flies like a ballerina

*

My heart is still young
Which sings
in spite of the passing of time
It keeps crying
And finds the ardent wait and desire
Dear being
I have been obsessed by you since childhood
It's not enough for you
that I give my last breath...,
You are not satisfied with my death's drunkeness
There again I found my sanctuary
In the arms of an eternal love
Like a night
From The Thousand and One Nights
generous as a drunk in ecstasy
To give without expecting a return
Love is the child of a generous gift
O beauty of this love
It takes nothing from you except passion and madness

But can a lover delight in torture?
As if love was a means of giving you soul
But what love is this!
Recognising it gives itself entirely with generosity
to the drunk and the magician.
And it sees in its death a spell
Dear lover, are you still a servant

At the heart of the beloved café?
And do you rejoice at the hymn if an eternal voice
Which becomes immortal?

*

I am against the current
I make water spurt from stones
If I'm allowed
I transform the impossible into reality
Why does the destiny of sincere and honest people
become poverty and injustice the gagged
mouth and the stifled voice
Towards which god, which throne
do we turn our eyes?
In what church, which synagogue, which mosque
are we going to complain about our situation?
I intended to be a dervish among the
searchers after truth to affront injustice
with will and determination
but they said to me You are still too young
to bang the tambourine.
So get together with God's hermitage
and take a good look
today the throne god
is up for auction
by the traders in religion
the charlatans
and perhaps the dervish's song
is made of vows upon the Torah, the Bible and the Koran
They too are up for auction
because all the gods are in Satan's goblet
at the hypocritical drinkers' banquet
they too are deaf
mute and blind.

Shahnizas Rachid

The Refugee

On the earth
He had a speck of ground and a foot
They sold him and cut off his foot
In the air
He had an oxygen atom and a lung
Breathe in and empty his lungs
In life
He had an iota of dream and a desire
They crushed him and killed his hopes

He went to other countries
That provides dust, air and dreams
But
Without a foot, how to trample the earth?
Without a lung, how to breathe the air?
Without desire, how to realise your dream?

Two Stars and a Sun

Don't talk to me about stars at night
You give them to my eyes
I want the two stars
The two squares in your face's sky
And this wakened night
In a distracted look!
Don't promise me the morning sun
You put it between my palms
I want this sun
The elasticity between your ribs
And this
morning which rises When you say:
'I love you.'

Solo

You are from there
I'm from here
But...
There's nothing strange between us
.....
I am there
Read the history of your town
So it's
among its stones in an ancient wall
that I've stayed there
Try to pronounce words with your accent
I laugh at your surprise
You think I grew up with you!
I was born here
I wore the same clothes as your mother
I see you attached to me like her dress
You held, little one!

*

There you are
Joy in my spoken or withheld words
The smiling town hall is there
It tells of your joy!

The Meeting Topples

I climb into my hammock
Send me towards the sky
I know my feet are light
You will return to touch the soil
Which haunts me
It is so high
Enough to convince me I'm a bird

*

I light the heart's fire
and I put memory's saucepan on it
I am going to cook a past which doesn't extinguish
and which doesn't burn
So the odour of nostalgia propagates in the soul
and I become human again
What is a human being
without nostalgia?

*

Every autumn a tree with innocent leaves asks, 'Why?'
Each hunt a dove with free wings asks, 'Why?'
Each bullet a sky of pure colours asks 'Why?'
Each war an ancient land asks, 'Why?'
Each dove a sincere heart asks, 'Why?'
And the response is a distant dream
that the question's eyes don't see!

Fatma Savci

You call me from afar

You call me from afar
Let me light the candle
I'm going to ferment the grapes in the pit
     to welcome you to the sunsets
Leave this dream at the foot of the mountain
     you've watered with our blood
You are like a gentle wind in the branches
     of the poplar

You call me
If you were a little needle, every morning
     you would embroider for me a Herîrî land
If you were a stream, you would carry me
     on your women's shoulders which breastfeed
as far as the sea and you would be happy about my existence

In the mortal wait, the time of commandment has come
It's seven centuries since with forgetfulness
     it rained in the desert
Escaping malediction, I accompanied the night's passengers
     with the song of the dengbej
Put on your blue scarf for the journey

You see now I'm a drop of silver water near Ispahan
My clothes held up by the torrent in an unfulfilled love
I am a wound which must be stitched
I miss running, setting free from his green carpet this horse
Another dawn appears with this hymn, get rid of your
        fur-lined coat before the moon
People aren't afraid, ever. They pitch their black tents
        on the plain and they light the Zoroastrian flame.
The naked dagger is the place of death and it's a hundred
        years since it has looked at me
Who knows I'm the associate of this fallen star or a ruined
        castle in history's memory of women.

Gazelle and Peace Pipe

The flower emerges gently
for a moment it plunges its pistil in the kohl
to decorate its eyes
The door's key opens
An angry wind throws before him butterfly flowers
Struck by their difficult autumn
A chick collapses before its silence
Her ear is pricked
Still from afar she hears the sound of black destiny
She empties her mouth of her mother's words and complaints

The box of kohl the dawn
and the lantern
fall from her trembling hands
onto the blue carpet
with the clack of the shuttle.

They take the red veil
Off the head of a gazelle from the plain
with captive eyes in its pomegranate face

Like a trembling slaughtered lamb
Its last words
Between its cherry-red lips;
'Don't touch my heart.
From my bones make peace pipes.'

The Sound of the Flute

After the flood, a wave hits history's banks
The sound of the flute comes from the coffee-maker
A blonde takes out a heart with a handle on the left
and puts it onto the golden plate, where the cup of coffee
      should be

Soon she will pass in front of the tribe's heroes with her tray
she knows the one holding out his hands towards
      the red hyacinth cup
For the first gulp of coffee
Is heading off towards a country where her beloved
      is trapped by a wolf
He emigrates
And opens the door to his death and his beloved

He sees the heart of this blond is an ivy
Which pursues the sword's noise and passes
      towards Leylan hill
With its covers of gold and olive-black, to Lake Hatun
In the pain of waiting, he forgets it

Fringe and tress
Set fire to an epic history howling
It's a flower's word in eruption for the house's beauty
Which cries: Enough of the seven Apocalypses!

For this blonde's mourning, the girl
Falls on a distant land

She hasn't even a bit of beeswax
nor an evil eye's pearl to put on her forehead

There's nothing she can do
She gives her last fur-lined coat to Edul
While death's fever arrives
She wraps Gogerçin the chevalier
so his soul and his injured body will not fall

His soul, dead love's residue
floats above the tents of the Kikan and Milan tribes
In front, the fire for the coffee
Is like a bleating lamb

She understands she will never wake
Her path is more difficult
And her wound which doesn't bleed
The mulberry's shadow hasn't yet fallen on her killers
The blood of one history must pass to another

No, she isn't going towards Erdul
Towards the place where there's a tomb with an Arab name
And a wife whose wings are broken
Recognising in the black snake on the door of Lalişa Nûranî
Long live salvation!

A Gazelle Sleeps on a Cave's Rock

I'm the daughter of sacred fire
Time has passed
You don't know you must cut my cord
Don't ask the caravans of mourning today where
            the sun's door is
They've forgotten their rare morning songs

Look at the Berivan, those who are stuck in mourning
Their handkerchiefs don't get to the shepherds
Thise who have grief, in which castle will they arrive?

The sound of the payziokan songs no longer rises
            from the valley
who knows, those lovers, where do they hide
            in the plains their stars' canvas

Is it love?
On Yelda's night, does he come back in a
            pomegranate flower?

You will no longer wake at this distance
I'm tired looking for your face in the snow
No, the verse can't be read in this cold
The greenery covers the countryside in solitude

I'm inflamed in the mauve night and no longer want
            to extinguish myself
when this gazelle sleeps alone on the cave rock.

Maryam Sheikho

I feel as if thousands of people inhabit me

I feel as if thousands of people inhabit me
They walk beneath my skin
Their steps hurt me
They share my breath
My inhalation has become shameful
Expiration...I yawned...
It begins to drive me mad
These people lead a normal
Life They wake me at
Midnight because of their party's racket
They remove me from my work to fall asleep
And I become pale and cold
I'm tired of their long walks
My feet will no longer tolerate
All these shoes
Even my ears are closed, for an indeterminate time
The internal voices have saturated them
I don't stop thinking
Histories I haven't lived
Preoccupy me

*

I feel I can fly away –
I head towards the balcony and I try...
It's sure, there are birds which inhabit me
I throw myself in a swimming pool
I try to save
the fish who are in me
*

Yesterday I made a mistake
Instead of taking off my shirt
I tore off my skin
I would have liked to meet them
But I saw no one
I hit my chest
And I shouted
Anyone there?
GREAT BURST OF LAUGHTER which lasts
For minutes, hours, days, years
And no response
except for their wrinkles which start to appear on my face

*

You the stranger
show me your face.
You are as pale as a dream
Feeble and yellow as death
As distant as life.
As full of truth as a lie
Come and sit near to me
We can sit on a single chair,
I'm the lady of nothingness
Lay down at my feet
Like an autumn leaf
I'm going to drown you in a glass of water
Which I'll drink in the morning,
I'm going to be full of you
It will be enough for life to continue to bloom
In a bedroom
Without doors
Without windows.

Mahuin Shekralpour

Until Liberation

Nothing remains
of the rain and wind's agitated songs
of the charming dance of thousands of autumn leaves'
nothing remains
to cut the heart of the town's sycamores
Good news to walk once more
on the rustling leaves
We have survived
With windblown hair
in the blackness
With the woman's cry for a free life
until the emergence of the love
which hasn't stayed without a reply
We have survived

Autumn and its Red Pomegranates

Autumn isn't the season for dying
in my land's blind blackness
The girls have fallen to the ground
for the song
a dance, a smile
What is their paradise
Tearing up their virginity was useless
Before hanging this autumn
It's not the season for dying
now
Red pomegranate seeds
Life's cry
which crosses terror's desert
This autumn isn't the season for dying
for bleeding pomegranates,
for the yellow leaves and for girls
until liberation

Rudi Suleiman

Write

Write
On the autumn leaves
On the fridge magnets
Between the lines of false history
On the shirt of a friend sitting in front of you in class
On the school's walls
On the corners of avenues full of encounters with onlookers
Write
With the blood of your lover
On the dress of the dancers while they tremble for you
On the repeated stories of grandmothers
In the notebooks
And on the file of the account books
Between the pages of the grocery debts
On the wings of butterflies
In front of the scarecrows in the fields
Between the lines of the semis
Of the wind, the air, the sky and the sea
Write
It doesn't matter what you write
On your ex-girlfriends
The beautiful and the ugly
Attached to the devotion to your obscurity
Write
For life on death
For death on life
For the present on tomorrow
For tomorrow on the past
Write
With transparent ink in the air

With the dust accumulated on the lorry's windscreen
On the curtains of luxury hotels
And the mirrors of beautiful women
with red lips
with pens
with water
ink
with saliva
on everything
Write
and so what you write
might have a flavour and a colour
the flavour of each time you end
Attach to your writing the picture of a heart
It doesn't matter how the days pass,
aday will come which will lean gently towards you
and tap you on the shoulder like a mother
O great child.

Autumn My Friend

Autumn
Point your arm towards the sky
Because there's a corpse which arrives
She visits a little girl who has lost her heart in a war
kill her
and then let's sit face to face
to kill the remains of death on
this earth.

Confusion

O walls which fall

Are you always faithful to your curvature

O homeless mornings don't learn the news in bulk

Take them as they are with newspapers which twist the
tongue when there's a mass slaughter.

Your fishing is more than a feeling dispersed behind
           your cut tongue

Oh God

Are you still there, because the suspicion of a question like
           this one is an apostasy
Many questions like this one make each time
a noise which explodes in the brain cells

O, friend
Are you well?
I look for you still in the days' ruins

How can a torrent sweep your white heart and which curses
           don't bow before you?

O, tomb
where is my father?

Me, for 312 days I have woken up in the morning
to drink coffee

I mow the grass in my heart and what is round about
I call it often as though it didn't hear me
Since when has death not listened to her orphans?

Meryem Temir

It Could

It could have been
The bullet was a bird
The bomb a dove
Your hand ivy
The artillery a kite
And your mouth a fishing net

You might not have taken your distance
To leave me here footless
Walking without laughing in the streets
It might have been
A blue eye on our neighbours' balcony
A little puppy taking refuge in the shadow of a wall
fearing the sound of passers-by's steps
I could have
put you in a wooden box which I would have
closed with ninety-nine locks
without letting the breeze go through you!
You could
have left the door ajar
for a laugh
which would change the plans of the great powers
the influx of refugees
the murder of unarmed civilians
the orphaning of children

It could have been before you left
I put you
on guard, war has no pity for our dry
Hearts!

War

The one-armed child
Wakes every morning
From the nightmare of his house being bombed
He looks at his mother in the tent
Wiping with the right side of her torn shawl
The tears from her left-eye
He says with the impotence of a man of ninety
'Mum... the war has broken my back.'

Panic will leave the children's eyes
It will turn its back and walk
The war which took you from me
Is going to turn its back and go away
Treacherous like a man who has stabbed his wife
Forty-four times

The road likes the passers-by
The road embraces the children's steps
The children who have lost
Their feet in the war
It has been devoured by the explosion of shells
your hand which caressed my hair
every day
in a war which doesn't worry about anyone
As if the house that we will not build
does not have any doors
any windows
a back garden
vulnerable to the shells

The missiles you won't fire
The shells you won't fire
The house we won't build
The houses are for the children's hearts
The houses are not for canon.

Forty Years

Women say to me
'Don't say how old you are.'
Then I smile forty smiles
I hold my hand toward the clouds
I have forty unfinished
sobs
Forty tears which didn't fall
But I have your hands... forty years to come
And to throw on all this hatred
Forty stones

Nothing Changes

Here nothing changes
The governor
The Party secretary
The departmental director
Dad's anger and mum's submission
My children's malice
The dustbins and the crevices in the streets
The men who see women as fruits
Whose varieties they must taste
Here nothing moves
Except the death-counter
It is like a man
A man of seventy
Who cuts down lives without stopping.

Don't Panic

Don't panic if you wake in the morning
And see that all the town's trees look like your shadow
The roses like your cheeks
The squares like your heart
And your eyes like burning lamps

Don't panic if I forget all the words
By repeating your name without power or force.
Don't panic if you see your face in the evening
Instead of the moon
And your fingers in the place of stars

Don't panic and I cry in your absence
as if it was the last day of my life
Don't panic if I insist
That your chest is a town and that
Your lashes can kill me
although my mind is healthy.

Hevin Temmo

What Are Men Looking For?

What are men looking for
If they came back at night
A yellow desire on a bamboo bed
Motherly breasts
Stored in a cupboard
The thin ribs of a lonely woman
Or a stressful desire to fall asleep with no concern
For the solitude which grows by itself in the mirror

*

What are men looking for?
The visible scars on the women
Trying to make of them a strangled hymn with grapes
Which possess a nutritional value like vitamins, for example
O, to make themselves invisible, so they can be swallowed
          by plants submerged in saliva

*

The curtains give themselves up to the colour of the infinite
And in the salty morning is inexplicable
And the foetus which kicks me without stopping
Seems to be hidden
Inside a basket of grapes

Like a child

I thought the dead were sleeping
Mad sleepers
As sleep comes, as it will in a tunnel dug in haste
And the cats miaow in the garden of the abandoned house
The winters which pass in the high country
Deceive the fatherland's truth about an annual funeral census
To the point it doesn't even know where to throw the dead
who don't mix
In its forgotten cupboards or in its dissimulated debris
in darkness's folds...
When you are left alone, you realize that tears are born from
the handle of the door which can be opened...
The departure door has no teeth
Except that its affliction's music flowers still in the hedges,
forgetting's tree which is touched by tiredness

Mountain Girls

The girl who smiles
In her wide trousers and her military shirt
Put her memory
Her family photos
And the poems from her town near her weapon
And many, many wishes on satin ribbons to hang
On the branches of the olive tree
When the girl forgets women's secrets
The dates of their monthly mood-swings
And the odour of a man when love passes with a laugh
It's this same girl
who gives out the beating of her pulse down there
in the mountains
Like a Kurdish string of beads around her neck
Like a dream which breathes in the war's ribs
with a song about this country
while she is without military boots.

*

The Kurd, on his way to the cemetery
has passed all the bullets
and the prophecies all the
languages and all the sky's
corridors and he hasn't
fallen alone into the water into
a dirtied pit.

Axin Wallat

Love and War

Nothing which goes on outside turns me away from you
All that turns in my head
and in the neighbours' heads
and the heads severed for the spectacle
or the one the swordsman shoots
into on freedom's terrain...
This spit that the world has received
from the head carried by criminal hands
it's that which makes me think endlessly
of you

*

At a certain time
we were innocent
very innocent
I bought the world for five lira
On the morning of the celebration
I reinforced it with my breath in a red balloon
and when the balloon deflated
I found myself alone
in the world I didn't know
and which didn't know me

*

The child on the bike
is no longer astonishing
Neither the train on the rails
nor the man
nor the woman
are astonishing
nor everything which belongs to them
Little by little
the plane becomes like a bird
the boat like a fish
and the army like ants

But war?
Nothing look like war
except human beings
Nothing looks like this morning
Its coldness doesn't look like departure
I don't feel a loss of anyone
I have nostalgia for nothing
Light, I am

There is no past which doesn't cause me grief
no future which doesn't worry me
with fears of the moment
I love and I detest everyone
equally
I belong to nothing and no one
belongs to me I wait for news
I see many bodies across the screen
many who drowned this morning
and the night before

The musician has stopped playing
and the singer hasn't covered her stomach
with the folds of her dress

light, light I walk
no fatherland on my shoulder
no children's cries
no women who ruin my tranquillity
no men who incite my curiosity
no old people who provoke my compassion
they are all free now
all dead
in the last explosion

Tugce Eve Yasar

To Those Who Ask for Anatolia

We are sitting with my grandfather
On the vast plateau, on the roots of the only tree
This apple tree which matures its scarlet fruit
Before us stretches out the Kose mountains
We are in a village in Anatolia
My grandfather's children were born in this village
He is tired
He has just mown the lawn
A wasp flies around us
My grandfather accompanies its buzzing
with a popular tune
I ask him
'What was that story? Tell me again grandfather.'
'Do you mean the Ode to Earth?'
'The Ode to Earth.'
'My grandfather's children were born in this village.'
He rolls a cigarette,
'You will also be among the insulted,' he says,
'Your friends will be pitiless and apparently friendly traitors,
These ugly men you don't know and who diverge from the
        laws. Those who know neither the heights of the
        Kizilirmak,
Nor our Ahmed Arif,
Nor Kul Himmet's poetry...
You will be among the insulted
And your cocoons will be destroyed.'
I stay at his left
I play with the earth
My grandfather hugs my shoulders
'My grandfather's children were born in this village.'
'And what must we do grandfather?'

He looks at the earth on my hands
'Listen,' he says,
'Listen. Your hands will better hold your pen
They will hang on zealously to life
To your hair
To your fingers
They will grip
They will seize it by its wrists, my little one!
Because spring will return
Spring will return.'
My grandfather's children were born in this village.
Henceforth we'll sing for the earth
For the earth which grows day by day
However, hang on to life
Grip its hands, its hair!
Seize it by the wrist.
We sing once more for the earth
Now the spring approaches
While our cocoons are destroyed
While the insulted besiege us, We
Sing once more for the earth
Above all, don't forget!

For Those Who Can't Break Out of Their Cocoon

What must we put up with to not grieve?
If the sea's waves mount
To the fine blue end,
Beyond the rocks...
To say 'we are children of the same era'
and to distance ourselves from one another?
To knit meshes of time
From my heart towards yours...

What must we put up with so as not to grieve?
If the fire foams at the summit of the mountainous lands
To their peak...
To say 'My heart has no room to suffer in my chest'
and to smother the words which haven't yet seen winter?
To take separate paths from my palms towards your hands?
What must we put up with not to grieve?
If the afternoon wind dances
On the Sahara Desert
On today's past and even yesterday's...
To say 'happiness is far from us'
And to gird oneself by silence?
To multiply the rivers of rain from your eyes towards mine?

Of course, you knew it well
The absolute truth
The discreet sea has never given up its waves
On the pretext it is agitated, furious
The sea is untamed, independent – of course
But the essential is it can't help itself
from embracing the learned mountain's
rebellious maverick fire
The storm? That, it's overwhelming, without pity, you know
The desert, delicate.
However,

However, they didn't come back even once against their wind
– You know it all right.
Come out of your cocoon!

Time's Windmill

I woke suddenly
Beyond the window
The sky showed its healing wound
Among the clouds,
A very light bleeding, blue
Was it a dream?
You were smiling –
I can't recall exactly. Your
Smile was like the dolphins' smile.
Your eyes, your lips like a line, fine.
In the untidiness of my stuffy room
To lean on the sky's blue wound
I set about looking for a handkerchief...
For an instant, I heard your voice,
I fixed myself there, so not to lose it.
The sky's wound bleeds still.
It's four in the morning, the room is black
However I close my eyes
To put my palms on your sigh
I take a step towards her
I take a step towards your voice,
The murmur of your silence...
The murmur of your silence!
– I smile.
Now the day breaks
Outside strike days
The railway workers keep guard at day break,
The yellow jackets embrace the ardour of the strike
On the outskirts of town,
In the fifty-sixth week
Soon, uncles with uniforms and truncheons
Will wake from their rusty sleep.
I moan, 'The Revolution obeys no calendar,'
I scratch in my turn the sky's wound

– it bleeds.
In this town, the early risers are the birds
In all seasons.
And me too,
The swallows whine something
A blue wound moves.

Notes

'Towns'
Fariyad is a Kurdish name.

'All the village came together here'
Sultana and Rehana were two women who were killed to cleanse the honour of their village.

'Letters dampened by tears'
Sinjar is a town in Northern Iraq, formerly home to many Yazidis. In 2014 Daesh/ISIS slaughtered 5k Yazidis in Sinjar, forcing thousands of women into sexual slavery and sending half a million refugees into exile.

'You call me from afar'
The Herîrî were a Kurdish tribe that flourished during the Ottoman period. Dengbej are Kurdish traditional singers.

'The Sound of the Flute'
Edul is a legendary love-lorn shepherd. Gogercin (Dove) was the name of his horse. Lalişa Nûranî is a mountain valley in Iraq, and the site of the Yazidi's holiest temple.

'A Gazelle Sleeps on a Cave's Rock'
Berivan are women who milk lambs in the mountains
Yelda's night is 21 December, a Yazidi night of prayer and celebration.

'To those who ask for Anatolia'
The Kizilirmak is the longest river in Turkey. Ahmed Arif (1927-1991) was a Turkish-Kurdiish poet. Kul Himmet was a sixteenth-century Alevi-Bektashi folk poet.

The Poets

Kajal Ahmad was born in 1967 in Kirkuk, Iraq. She is a poet, social critic, television-presenter and the editor of *Kurdistan News*.

Amira Khaled Al-Abdiko is a Yazidi poet from Barchira in the Nenoua region. She was born in 2001 and is a member of the poetry group Barchira.

Sara Aktas was born in 1976. She studied philosophy in Ankara. She spent ten years in Turkish prisons because of her membership of the PKK. In 2004 she was released, and became part of the Women's Council of the Kurdish Democratic Socialist Party. Her first book of poems was published while she was in prison.

Khonav Ayoub was born in Syria. She studied at the University of Tishreen in Latakia and at the university of Euphrates. In 2013, she emigrated to Iraqi Kurdistan, where she works as a school-teacher.

Lara Ayoub currently lives in Düsseldorf. She has recently published a novel about the Syrian diaspora.

Ronak Aziz has a degree from the Academy of Fine Arts, Baghdad. She had six solo exhibitions in Baghdad and worked as director of the Degal Art Association in Kirkuk. She now lives in Gothenburg.

Wiam Badrakhan is a Syrian artist and a photographer. During the Syrian civil-war she recorded the sufferings of civilians in her murals on the walls of Homs.

Kosert Ahmed Bakes began writing as a teenager. After the 1991 uprising, she worked as a journalist. A member of the Academy for Politics and Democratic Thought, she has published and translated several books.

Nazand Begikhan is a poet and visiting professor in the Vincent Wright Chair at Sciences-Po, Paris. The editor-in-chief of the Kurdish edition of the *Monde diplomatique*, she has written eight collections of poetry in Kurdish, French and English and translated Eliot and Baudelaire into Kurdish.

Leyla Mexo Berazi was born in Batman in Turkey. She studied Folklore and Ethnology at Ankara University.

Yara Biran was born in Kobani, Syria. She now lives in Germany where she works for the social-welfare organisation Diakonie Deutschland.

Simin Cayci was born in Iran. When she as 29 she was driven out of teaching by the Iranian government, imprisoned and exiled. Many of her poems have been made into songs and recorded by Kurdish singers. She is a member of Kurdish PEN.

Majda Dari was born in Syria. She studied Philosophy in Damascus. She now lives in the USA. She has published poetry, essays and a novel.

Sarwin Darwish was born in Erbil, Iraq in 1974. She has published two collections of poetry.

Avin Kissra Mahmoud (Dibo) was born in Syria. She has worked as a teacher and in public relations management. She is involved with an orphan's organisation in Syria and works as an interpreter for an NGO working with refugee families.

Tarifa Dusky (real name Maryman Ali) was born in 1974. She has been a member of the Dohuk union of writers since 2000. She's published three books of poetry.

Elham Erfan was born in 1980 in Iran. She teaches at Teheran University.

Roonak Faradji is a poet and journalist from Iran. She studied English and translation at Azad University and obtained a doctorate in child protection from the Iranian Academy.

Mizgin Hasko was born in Syria in 1973. She has written eight collections of poetry.

Maha Hassan is a journalist and novelist from Aleppo. Her work was banned in Syria. Since 2004 she has lived in France.

Fatema Hersan was born in northern Syria. She has worked as a teacher of Arabic in secondary schools in Qamishi and Raqqa. In 2001 she emigrated to Sweden, where she founded the Kurdish society for language and culture.

Bahar Hossein was born in 1983 in Iran. She holds a degree in Persian language and literature. In 2010, for political reasons, she moved to Iraqi Kurdistan, where she worked as a radio presenter. She now lives in Germany.

Rehab Fawaz Hussein was born in 1989 near Mosul.

Even Ibrahim grew up in Damascus. She has published five collections. Since 2000 she has lived in the USA, where she works with children with Special Needs.

Vian Juma was born in 1983 in a village near Mosul. She is a founder member of the Bashiqa Writers' Union.

Xunav Kano was born in Syria in 1993. She studied Arab languages and literature at Al-Furtat University. She now lives in Germany.

Rogen Kedo was born in Syria in 1982. She currently lives in Germany, where she works as a poet and musician.

Fadwa Kilani was born in Syria. She is a member of the executive committee of Kurdistan journalists and head of public relations at Voice of the Detained. She has published four poetry collections. She lives in the UAE.

Dunea Al Marchawi was born in 1975 in Iraq. She lives in Bahzani in northern Iraq.

Bejan Matur was born in 1961 in southern Turkey to an Alevi family. After law studies in Ankara, she founded and directed the Diyarbakar Arts and Culture Foundation. A selection of her poems is published in English, *In the Temple of a Painted God* (Arc 2004).

Widad Nabi studied economics at the University of Aleppo. She has published three collections in Arabic. She lives in Berlin where she writes for Arab and German magazines.

Narin Omar was born in Syria. Married with three children, she has won several prizes including the Jakor Khan.

Koestan Omarzedeh was born in Iran. Her family was forced to leave Iran when she was a child. She has lived in Europe for twenty-two years. She now works as a teacher and interpreter for refugees.

Sarwah Osman Mustafa was born in 1966 in Kirkuk. She grew up in a communist family. She lives in Erbil where she works in a school, and is an active member of the Kurdish National Congress.

Shahnizas Rachid was born in Damascus. She is the director of the Arab language department at the International School of Choueifat in Erbil.

Fatma Savci is a Yazidi poet, born in Turkey in 1974. After fighting with the PKK, she was imprisoned for many years. Following her release in 2003 she worked as a television and print journalist, and published books of poetry and history books. She now lives in Sweden.

Maryam Sheikho was born in 1986. She has taught at the University of Fine Arts in Damascus and has published four collections of poetry.

Mahuin Shekralpour was born in 1964 in Iran. Involved in Kurdish politics when she was a teenager, she was first imprisoned when she was just seventeen. Later, she was involved in the Komala Party of Iranian Kurdistan, becoming an officer in the Komela Peshmerga. In 1987 she and her husband and children were imprisoned. Her husband died under torture in prison.

Rudi Suleiman was born in Aleppo in 1984. She studied music and writes poetry and fiction. She now lives in Amsterdam.

Meryem Temir was born in 1979. She has published several collections of poetry. She lives in Syria.

Hevin Temmo was born in Syria. She has a degree in philosophy from the University of Aleppo university. After the assassination of her father, she emigrated with her family to Germany.

Axin Wallat was born in Aleppo. She studied Arabic literature at Damascus University, and has published eight books in Kurdish.

Tugce Eve Yasar was born in 1994 in Turkey. She studied in Istanbul and in Paris, where she currently lives.

The Translators

Sara Aktas' 'When Senem Hung Herself from the Paradise Tree' was translated from Kurmandji into French by Sabahattin Kayhan.

Kosert Ahmed Bakes' 'A simple sneeze and life is over' was translated from Arabic into French by Muhammad Hussein al-Muhandis.

Nazand Begikhani's 'Evening on the Loire' was translated into French by the author.

Leyla Mexo Berazî's 'Serenity of the Flowers' was translated from Kurmandji into French by Sabahattin Kayhan.

Sîmîn Caycî's 'Town' was translated from Sorani into French by Judy Tarboush.

Elham Erfan's 'The trees tremble under the bastard brambles' was translated from Farsi into French by Firoozeh Radj and Jean-Louis Cloet.

Mizgin Hasko's 'The Earth's Angels' was translated from Arabic into French by Ibrahim A-Youssef.

Bahar Hossein's 'They will never be closed' was translated from Arabic into French by Hafiz Abdul Rahman; 'Poem' was translated from Sorani by Judy Tarboush.

Fatma Savci's 'A Gazelle Sleeps on a Cave's Rock' was translated from Kurmandji into French by Sabahattin Kayhan.

The three poems by Tugce Eve Yasar were translated from Turkish into French by Baris Berhamoglu.

All the other poems were translated into French by Maram al-Masri.

All poems translated into English by Alan Dent.